Step-by-Step
PROBLEM SOLVING

Grade 6

Frank Schaffer
An imprint of Carson-Dellosa Publishing LLC
Greensboro, North Carolina

Credits

Content Editor: Christine Schwab
Copy Editor: Sandra Ogle
Layout and Cover Design: Lori Jackson

 This book has been correlated to state, common core state, national, and Canadian provincial standards. Visit *www.carsondellosa.com* to search for and view its correlations to your standards.

Copyright © 2012, SAP Group Pte Ltd

Frank Schaffer
An imprint of Carson-Dellosa Publishing LLC
PO Box 35665
Greensboro, NC 27425 USA
www.carsondellosa.com

ISBN 978-1-609964-81-8
01-335111151

Introduction

The **Step-by-Step Problem Solving** series focuses on the underlying processes and strategies essential to problem solving. Each book introduces various skill sets and builds upon them as the level increases. The six-book series covers the following thinking skills and heuristics:

Thinking Skills:
- ❏ Analyzing Parts and Wholes
- ❏ Comparing
- ❏ Classifying
- ❏ Identifying Patterns and Relationships
- ❏ Deduction
- ❏ Induction
- ❏ Spatial Visualization

Heuristics:
- ❏ Act It Out
- ❏ Draw a Diagram/Model
- ❏ Look for a Pattern
- ❏ Work Backward
- ❏ Make a List/Table
- ❏ Guess and Check
- ❏ Before and After
- ❏ Make Suppositions
- ❏ Use Equations

Students who are keen to develop their abilities in problem solving will learn quickly how to:
- ❏ make sense of the problem sum: what am I asked to find?
- ❏ make use of given information: what do I know?
- ❏ think of possible strategies: have I come across similar problems before?
- ❏ choose the correct strategy: apply what I know confidently.
- ❏ solve the problem: work out the steps.
- ❏ check the Answer is the solution logical and reasonable?

Practice questions follow after each skill-set example, and three graded, mixed practices (easy, intermediate, challenging) are provided for an overall assessment of the skills learned. The worked solutions show the application of the strategies used. Students will find this series invaluable in helping them understand and master problem-solving skills.

S. Leong

Table of Contents

Strategy Summary

The following summary provides examples of the various skill sets taught in Step-by-Step Problem Solving.

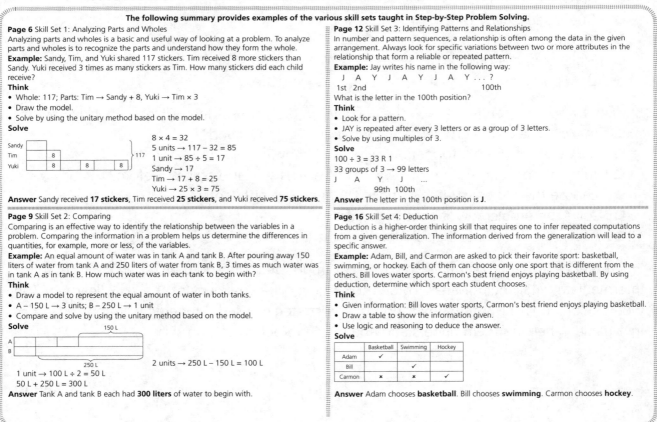

Page 6 Skill Set 1: Analyzing Parts and Wholes

Analyzing parts and wholes is a basic and useful way of looking at a problem. To analyze parts and wholes is to recognize the parts and understand how they form the whole.

Example: Sandy, Tim, and Yuki shared 117 stickers. Tim received 8 more stickers than Sandy. Yuki received 3 times as many stickers as Tim. How many stickers did each child receive?

Think
- Whole: 117; Parts: Tim → Sandy + 8, Yuki → Tim × 3
- Draw the model.
- Solve by using the unitary method based on the model.

Solve

Sandy
Tim 8
Yuki 8 8 8 } 117

$8 \times 4 = 32$
5 units → $117 - 32 = 85$
1 unit → $85 \div 5 = 17$
Sandy → 17
Tim → $17 + 8 = 25$
Yuki → $25 \times 3 = 75$

Answer Sandy received **17 stickers**, Tim received **25 stickers**, and Yuki received **75 stickers**.

Page 9 Skill Set 2: Comparing

Comparing is an effective way to identify the relationship between the variables in a problem. Comparing the information in a problem helps us determine the differences in quantities, for example, more or less, of the variables.

Example: An equal amount of water was in tank A and tank B. After pouring away 150 liters of water from tank A and 250 liters of water from tank B, 3 times as much water was in tank A as in tank B. How much water was in each tank to begin with?

Think
- Draw a model to represent the equal amount of water in both tanks.
- A – 150 L → 3 units; B – 250 L → 1 unit
- Compare and solve by using the unitary method based on the model.

Solve

150 L
A
B
250 L

2 units → $250\,L - 150\,L = 100\,L$
1 unit → $100\,L \div 2 = 50\,L$
$50\,L + 250\,L = 300\,L$

Answer Tank A and tank B each had **300 liters** of water to begin with.

Page 12 Skill Set 3: Identifying Patterns and Relationships

In number and pattern sequences, a relationship is often among the data in the given arrangement. Always look for specific variations between two or more attributes in the relationship that form a reliable or repeated pattern.

Example: Jay writes his name in the following way:

J A Y J A Y J A Y . . . ?
1st 2nd   100th

What is the letter in the 100th position?

Think
- Look for a pattern.
- JAY is repeated after every 3 letters or as a group of 3 letters.
- Solve by using multiples of 3.

Solve
$100 \div 3 = 33\ R\ 1$
33 groups of 3 → 99 letters
J   A   Y   J   ...
              99th 100th

Answer The letter in the 100th position is **J**.

Page 16 Skill Set 4: Deduction

Deduction is a higher-order thinking skill that requires one to infer repeated computations from a given generalization. The information derived from the generalization will lead to a specific answer.

Example: Adam, Bill, and Carmon are asked to pick their favorite sport: basketball, swimming, or hockey. Each of them can choose only one sport that is different from the others. Bill loves water sports. Carmon's best friend enjoys playing basketball. By using deduction, determine which sport each student chooses.

Think
- Given information: Bill loves water sports, Carmon's best friend enjoys playing basketball.
- Draw a table to show the information given.
- Use logic and reasoning to deduce the answer.

Solve

	Basketball	Swimming	Hockey
Adam	✓		
Bill		✓	
Carmon	✗	✗	✓

Answer Adam chooses **basketball**. Bill chooses **swimming**. Carmon chooses **hockey**.

Strategy Summary

Page 19 Skill Set 5: Induction

Induction is a reverse process of deduction. It is used to draw a general conclusion from specific computations in a problem.

Example: If ■ = 45, ● = 15, and ▲ = 20, fill in the blanks below with the same number to make the statement true.

■ = _____ × ▲ – _____ × ●

Think
• Gather clues from the information given.
• Use the clues to draw a general conclusion.

Solve

45 and 15 are odd numbers.
20 is an even number.

Possible answers:

45 = 3 × 20 – 1 × 15
(different numbers used, does not meet criteria)

odd = even – odd or odd – even
_____ × ▲ must be even because 20 is even.
45 = 9 × 20 – 9 × 15 (statement true)
So, ■ = _____ × ▲ – _____ × ●
   odd   even   odd

Answer So, ■ = **9** × ▲ – **9** × ●.

Page 22 Skill Set 6: Work Backward

Working backward is a strategy that makes use of the end result of a problem to find what it begins with. Very often, answers can be found by tracing back the steps and reversing the operations.

Example: Mia saved up some money for shopping. Her mother gave her $150 more. At a shop, Mia spent $80 on a bag and half of the remaining money on a pair of shoes. She was then left with $55. How much money did Mia save up?

Think
• Money left: $55
• Work backward by reversing the operations.

Solve

| $40 | $190 | $110 | $55 |

$55 × 2 = $110
$110 + $80 = $190
$190 – $150 = $40

Answer Mia saved up **$40**.

Page 25 Skill Set 7: Draw a Diagram/Model

Drawing diagrams helps us "see" the relationship among the data found in a problem. This is a good and effective way to organize information and data.

Example: A rectangular block of wood, 20 centimeters by 18 centimeters by 9 centimeters, is cut into many 3-centimeter cubes. What is the maximum number of 3-centimeter cubes that can be cut out?

Think
• Draw a block 20 cm by 18 cm by 9 cm.
• Draw 3-cm cubes within the block.
• Solve by using the diagram.

Solve

20 ÷ 3 = 6 R 2   (length)   ⇒ 6 cubes
18 ÷ 3 = 6   (width)   ⇒ 6 cubes
9 ÷ 3 = 3   (height)   ⇒ 3 cubes
6 × 6 × 3 = 108

Answer The maximum number of 3-centimeter cubes is **108**.

Page 28 Skill Set 8: Look for a Pattern

To make sense of the data given in a problem, examine the variables to find the specific pattern. The development of the pattern leads to a solution.

Example: Simone used some square blocks to build the figures shown below. How many square blocks does she need to build Figure 6?

Think
• Study the figures and look for a pattern.
• Draw a table to fill in the data.
• Use the table to find the solution.

Figure 1   Figure 2   Figure 3

Solve

Figure	Number of blocks	Pattern
1	1	1
2	3	1 + 2
3	6	1 + 2 + 3
4	10	1 + 2 + 3 + 4
⋮	⋮	⋮
6	21	1 + 2 + 3 + 4 + 5 + 6

Answer Simone needs **21 square blocks** to build Figure 6.

Page 31 Skill Set 9: Make a List/Table

Making a list or a table with the given data or information helps organize the data in an orderly manner. This makes it possible to see missing data or recognize patterns.

Example: Mrs. Toma bought some stickers for her students. If she gave each student 4 stickers, she would be 1 sticker short. If she gave each student 3 stickers, she would have 8 stickers left. How many students did she have altogether?

Think
• Data given: 4 stickers → 1 short (multiple of 4 less 1), 3 stickers → 8 left (multiple of 3 plus 8)
• List the multiples of 3 and 4.
• Find the common number.

Solve

Possible number of students:	1	2	3	4	5	6	7	8	⑨
Multiples of 4:	4	8	12	16	20	24	28	32	36
1 short:	3	7	11	15	19	23	27	31	㉟
Multiples of 3:	3	6	9	12	15	18	21	24	27
8 left:	11	14	17	20	23	26	29	32	㉟

Answer She had **9 students** altogether.

Page 34 Skill Set 10: Guess and Check

Guess and check refers to making calculated guesses and deriving a solution from them. It is a popular heuristic skill that is often used for upper primary mathematical problems. Because the guesses at the solutions can be checked immediately, the answers are always correct.

Example: Lucy was reading a book and stopped at 2 facing pages. The product of the 2 page numbers was 156. What were the page numbers?

Think
• Data: 2 page numbers are consecutive, product = 156
• Make guesses and list them.
• Check the solution and confirm the answer.

Solve

Guess 1: 10 × 11 = 110 ✗
Guess 2: 11 × 12 = 132 ✗
Guess 3: 12 × 13 = 156 ✓

Answer The page numbers were **12** and **13**.

Page 37 Skill Set 11: Before and After

Before and After is often used to solve problems with two scenarios. By putting the data into before and after diagrams or mathematical representations, and then doing a comparison, a solution can be derived easily.

Example: Mr. Unger had some American stamps and European stamps. The number of American stamps was $\frac{2}{3}$ that of European stamps. He gave some American stamps away, and the number of American stamps became $\frac{2}{5}$ that of European stamps. If he had 200 American stamps to begin with, how many of them did he give away?

Think
• Data: American stamps given away; European stamps remained unchanged.
• Make the ratio for European stamps the same before and after American stamps were given away.
• Solve by using the unitary method.

Solve

Before	After
Am : Eu	Am : Eu
2 : 3 ⎞×5	2 : 5 ⎞×3
10 : ⑮	6 : ⑮

10 – 6 = 4 units (American stamps given away)
10 units → 200
1 unit → 200 ÷ 10 = 20
4 units → 20 × 4 = 80

Answer He gave away **80 American stamps**.

Page 40 Skill Set 12: Make Suppositions

Making suppositions is another higher-order heuristic skill that is often used for upper primary mathematical problems. It requires one to make an assumption to a given problem before attempting to solve it.

Example: A farmer has 60 chickens and cows. They have a total of 144 legs. How many chickens does the farmer have?

Think
• Make assumptions that the farmer has either all chickens or all cows.
• Look for shortage or excess of legs and solve accordingly.

Solve

Assuming all are chickens:
total number of legs = 60 × 2 = 120
difference in total number of legs → 144 – 120 = 24 (excess)
difference in number of legs of chicken and cow → 4 – 2 = 2
cows → 24 ÷ 2 = 12
chickens → 60 – 12 = 48

Answer The farmer has **48 chickens**.

Skill Set 1: Analyzing Parts and Wholes

Analyzing parts and wholes is a basic and useful way of looking at a problem. To analyze parts and wholes is to recognize the parts and understand how they form the whole.

Example:

Sandra, Tia, and Yuri shared 117 stickers. Tia received 8 more stickers than Sandra. Yuri received 3 times as many stickers as Tia. How many stickers did each child receive?

💡 **Think**
- Whole: 117; Parts: Tia → Sandra + 8, Yuri → Tia × 3
- Draw the model.
- Solve by using the unitary method based on the model.

✏️ **Solve**

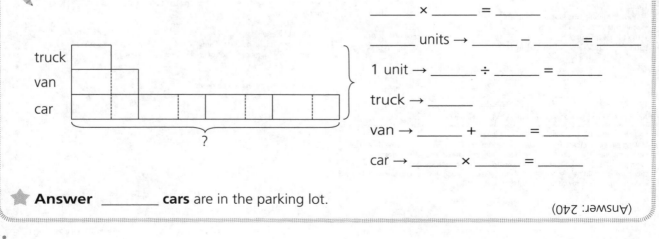

$8 \times 4 = 32$

5 units → $117 - 32 = 85$

1 unit → $85 \div 5 = 17$

Sandra → 17

Tia → $17 + 8 = 25$

Yuri → $25 \times 3 = 75$

⭐ **Answer** Sandra received **17 stickers**, Tia received **25 stickers**, and Yuri received **75 stickers**.

Give it a try!

A parking lot has 345 vehicles. It has 15 more vans than trucks. If the parking lot has 4 times as many cars as vans, how many cars are in the parking lot?

💡 **Think**

Fill in the data and solve by using the unitary method based on the model.

✏️ **Solve**

truck

van

car

?

_____ × _____ = _____

_____ units → _____ − _____ = _____

1 unit → _____ ÷ _____ = _____

truck → _____

van → _____ + _____ = _____

car → _____ × _____ = _____

⭐ **Answer** _____ **cars** are in the parking lot.

(Answer: 240)

Practice: Analyzing Parts and Wholes

1. Jenny, Lily, and Sasha shared 275 beads. Jenny received 25 more beads than Lily. Sasha received twice as many beads as Jenny. How many beads did Lily receive?

💡 **Think**

✏️ **Solve**

⭐ **Answer**

2. Factory A used 68 more gallons of water than factory B. Factory C used 4 times as much water as factory A. If the three factories used a total of 484 gallons of water, how much water did factory C use?

💡 **Think**

✏️ **Solve**

⭐ **Answer**

Practice: Analyzing Parts and Wholes

3. Ava, Lisa, Sally, and Raul shared a sum of $1,000. Ava received $12 more than Lisa. Sally received $16 more than Ava. Raul received twice as much money as Sally. How much money did Raul receive?

💡 **Think**

✏️ **Solve**

⭐ **Answer**

4. Bakery A used 12 fewer kilograms of flour than bakery B. Bakery C used twice as much flour as bakery A and bakery B combined. If the three bakeries used a total of 936 kilograms of flour, how much flour did bakery C use?

💡 **Think**

✏️ **Solve**

⭐ **Answer**

Skill Set 2: Comparing

Comparing is an effective way to identify the relationship between the variables in a problem. Comparing the information in a problem helps us determine the differences in quantities, for example, more or less, of the variables.

Example:

An equal amount of water was in tank A and tank B. After pouring away 150 liters of water from tank A and 250 liters of water from tank B, 3 times as much water was in tank A as in tank B. How much water was in each tank to begin with?

💡 **Think**
- Draw a model to represent the equal amount of water in both tanks.
- A – 150 L → 3 units; B – 250 L → 1 unit
- Compare and solve by using the unitary method based on the model.

✏️ **Solve**

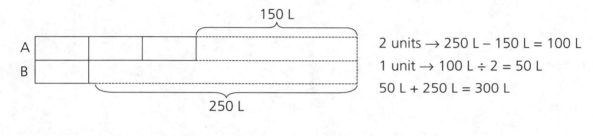

2 units → 250 L – 150 L = 100 L
1 unit → 100 L ÷ 2 = 50 L
50 L + 250 L = 300 L

⭐ **Answer** Tank A and tank B each had **300 liters** of water to begin with.

Give it a try!

Rope A and rope B were the same length. After 43 meters were cut from rope A, and 8 meters were cut from rope B, rope B became 6 times as long as rope A. What was the length of each rope to begin with?

💡 **Think**
Compare and solve by using the unitary method based on the model.

✏️ **Solve**

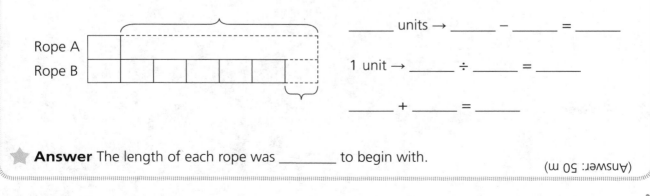

_____ units → _____ – _____ = _____

1 unit → _____ ÷ _____ = _____

_____ + _____ = _____

⭐ **Answer** The length of each rope was _____ to begin with.

(Answer: 50 m)

Practice: Comparing

1. Darius and Daniel each had an equal amount of money to spend. After Darius spent $360, and Daniel spent $150, Daniel had 8 times as much money as what Darius had left. How much money did each boy have to begin with?

💡 **Think**

✏️ **Solve**

⭐ **Answer**

2. Shane and Roberto shared a bag of marbles equally. After Shane lost 15 marbles in a game and Roberto lost 179 marbles, the number of marbles Shane had left was 5 times that of Roberto's. How many marbles were in the bag to begin with?

💡 **Think**

✏️ **Solve**

⭐ **Answer**

3. A fruit seller had the same number of apples and pears. After selling 82 apples and 34 pears, 4 times as many pears as apples were left. How many apples and pears did the fruit seller have to begin with?

💡 **Think**

✏️ **Solve**

⭐ **Answer**

4. An equal number of red and blue paper clips were in a box. After 57 red paper clips and 111 blue paper clips were used, 7 times as many red paper clips as blue paper clips were left. How many paper clips were in the box to begin with?

💡 **Think**

✏️ **Solve**

⭐ **Answer**

Skill Set 3: Identifying Patterns and Relationships

In number and pattern sequences, a relationship is often among the data in the given arrangement. Always look for specific variations between two or more attributes in the relationship that form a reliable or repeated pattern.

Example:

Jay writes his name in the following way:

J A Y J A Y J A Y ... ?
1st 2nd   100th

What is the letter in the 100th position?

 Think

- Look for a pattern.
- JAY is repeated after every 3 letters or as a group of 3 letters.
- Solve by using multiples of 3.

Solve

$$100 \div 3 = 33 \text{ R } 1$$

33 groups of 3 → 99 letters

J   A   Y   J   ...
                99th 100th

⭐ **Answer** The letter in the 100th position is **J**.

Give it a try!

Sam also writes his name in the same way:

S A M S A M S A M ... ?
                                    200th

What is the letter in the 200th position?

💡 **Think**

Solve again by using multiples of 3.

✏️ **Solve**

_____ ÷ 3 = _____ R _____

_____ groups of 3 → _____ letters

S   A   M   S   A   M   ...

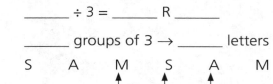

⭐ **Answer** The letter in the 200th position is _____.

(Answer: A)

Practice: Identifying Patterns and Relationships

1. Nora writes her name in the pattern below:

N O R A N O R A N O R A ... ?
1st 2nd   53rd

What is the letter in the 53rd position?

💡 **Think**

✏️ **Solve**

⭐ **Answer**

2. Ken writes some numbers in the pattern below:

1   2   3   3   2   1   1   2   3   ...   ?
1st 2nd   101st

What is the number in the 101st position?

💡 **Think**

✏️ **Solve**

⭐ **Answer**

3. Numbers are arranged in the table below. What number is X?

1st	2nd					12th
1	8	9	16	17	. . .	
2	7	10	15	18	. . .	X
3	6	11	14	19	. . .	
4	5	12	13	20	. . .	

 Think

Solve

Answer

Practice: Identifying Patterns and Relationships

4. Digits and letters are arranged in the pattern below:

   3　A　T　H　5　3　A　T　H　5　...　?
   1st　2nd　　　　　　　　　　　　　　88th

What is the digit or the letter in the 88th position?

💡 **Think**

✏️ **Solve**

⭐ **Answer**

5. Numbers on a piece of paper were arranged in columns A, B, C, D, E, and F. However, the paper was torn, and some numbers could not be seen. In which column would you expect to find 69?

💡 **Think**

A	B	C	D	E	F
1	2	3	4	5	6
12	11	10	9	8	7
13	14	15	16	17	18
24	23	22			

✏️ **Solve**

⭐ **Answer**

Skill Set 4: Deduction

Deduction is a higher-order thinking skill that requires you to infer repeated computations from a given generalization. The information derived from the generalization will lead to a specific answer.

Example:

Adam, Bill, and Carmon are asked to choose their favorite sport: basketball, swimming, or hockey. Each of them can choose only one sport that is different from the others. Bill loves water sports. Carmon's best friend enjoys playing basketball. By using deduction, determine which sport each student chooses.

Think

- Given information: Bill loves water sports, and Carmon's best friend enjoys playing basketball.
- Draw a table to show the information given.
- Use logic and reasoning to deduce the answer.

Solve

	Basketball	Swimming	Hockey
Adam	✓		
Bill		✓	
Carmon	✗	✗	✓

⭐ **Answer** Adam chooses **basketball**. Bill chooses **swimming**. Carmon chooses **hockey**.

Give it a try!

Three classmates, Leo, Mandy, and Noah, live in the same apartment building. They live on different floors: floor 4, floor 6, and floor 7. To meet his classmates on their floors, Leo has to take the elevator down. Noah lives on a floor between Leo and Mandy. On which floor does each student live?

Think

Use logic and reasoning to deduce the answer.

Solve

	Floor 4	Floor 6	Floor 7
Leo			
Mandy			
Noah			

⭐ **Answer** Leo lives on floor _____.

Mandy lives on floor _____.

Noah lives on floor _____.

(Answer: 7, 4, 6)

Practice: Deduction

1. Derek, Ellen, Felipe, and Jill are given seats P, Q, R, and S at a square table as shown. Ellen is seated on the left of Felipe and opposite Jill. Derek is seated at seat S, and all of the children are facing each other. Which seat is each student given?

💡 **Think**

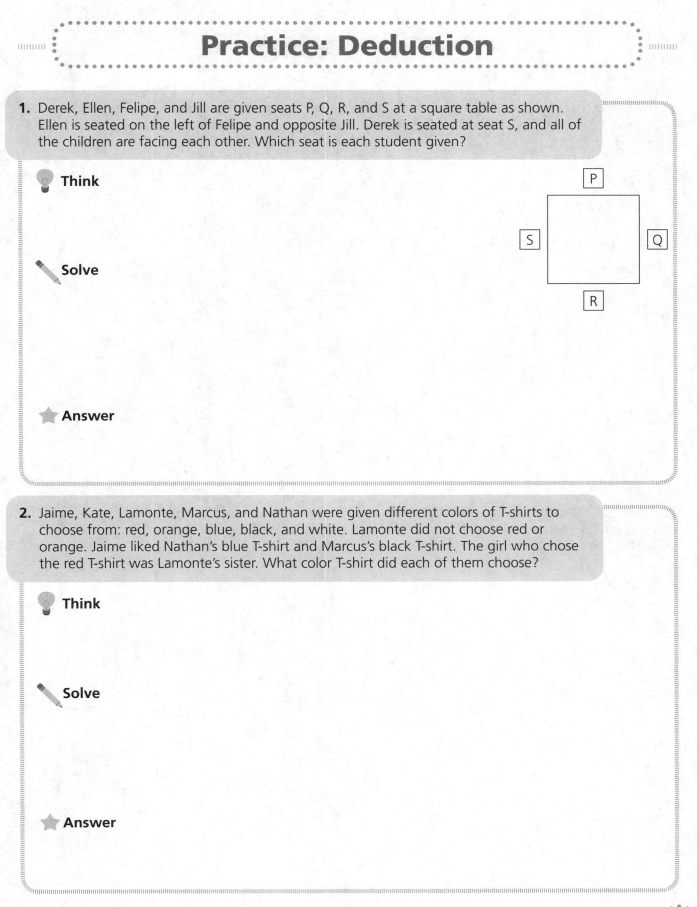

✏️ **Solve**

⭐ **Answer**

2. Jaime, Kate, Lamonte, Marcus, and Nathan were given different colors of T-shirts to choose from: red, orange, blue, black, and white. Lamonte did not choose red or orange. Jaime liked Nathan's blue T-shirt and Marcus's black T-shirt. The girl who chose the red T-shirt was Lamonte's sister. What color T-shirt did each of them choose?

💡 **Think**

✏️ **Solve**

⭐ **Answer**

Practice: Deduction

3. Five teams, A, B, C, D, and E, take part in a relay. Team A finishes before team E only and just behind team C. No team is before team B. What are the positions of the teams?

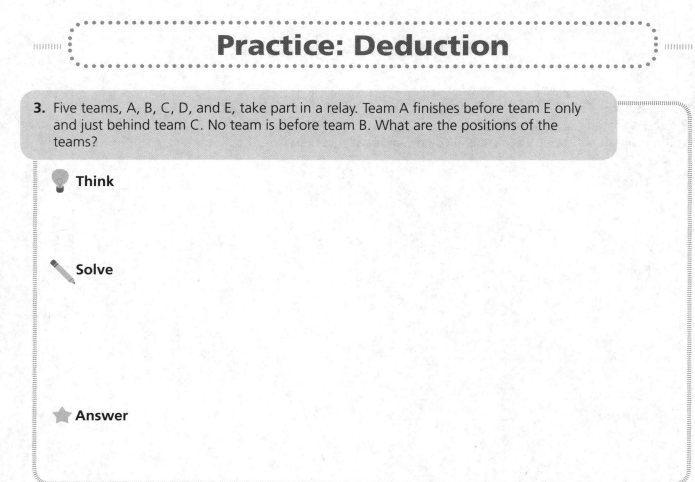

💡 **Think**

✏️ **Solve**

⭐ **Answer**

4. Among Mr. Lewis, Mr. Lang, and Mr. Taylor, one of them is a teacher. The other two are a doctor and a lawyer. Mr. Taylor is older than the lawyer. Mr. Lewis and the doctor are not the same age. The doctor is younger than Mr. Lang. Who is the teacher?

💡 **Think**

✏️ **Solve**

⭐ **Answer**

Skill Set 5: Induction

Induction is a reverse process of deduction. It is used to draw a general conclusion from specific computations in a problem.

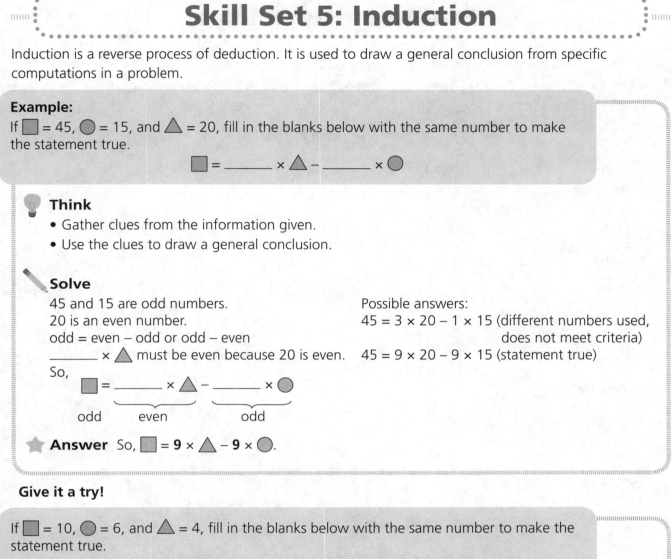

Example:

If ■ = 45, ◯ = 15, and ▲ = 20, fill in the blanks below with the same number to make the statement true.

$$■ = \underline{\hspace{1cm}} \times ▲ - \underline{\hspace{1cm}} \times ◯$$

💡 **Think**
- Gather clues from the information given.
- Use the clues to draw a general conclusion.

✏️ **Solve**

45 and 15 are odd numbers.
20 is an even number.
odd = even − odd or odd − even
$\underline{\hspace{1cm}} \times$ ▲ must be even because 20 is even.
So,

$$■ = \underline{\hspace{1cm}} \times ▲ - \underline{\hspace{1cm}} \times ◯$$
$\quad\quad$ odd $\quad$ even $\quad\quad\quad$ odd

Possible answers:
45 = 3 × 20 − 1 × 15 (different numbers used, does not meet criteria)
45 = 9 × 20 − 9 × 15 (statement true)

⭐ **Answer** So, ■ = **9** × ▲ − **9** × ◯.

Give it a try!

If ■ = 10, ◯ = 6, and ▲ = 4, fill in the blanks below with the same number to make the statement true.

$$■ = \underline{\hspace{1cm}} \div ▲ + \underline{\hspace{1cm}} \div ◯$$

💡 **Think**

Solve using clues from the information given.

✏️ **Solve**

10, 6, and 4 are all _____ numbers.
So,

$$■ = \underline{\hspace{1cm}} \div ▲ + \underline{\hspace{1cm}} \div ◯$$

⭐ **Answer** So, ■ = _____ ÷ ▲ + _____ ÷ ◯.

Practice: Induction

1. Given △ = 8, ◇ = 16, and ▢ = 4, fill in the blanks below with the same number to make the statement true.

◇ + ▢ = _____ × △ − _____ × ▢

💡 **Think**

✏️ **Solve**

⭐ **Answer**

2. Observe the following:

$$2 \times 9 = 18$$
$$22 \times 9 = 198$$
$$222 \times 9 = 1,998$$
$$2,222 \times 9 = 19,998$$

What can you induce from the number of 2s and the number of 9s? What is the result of $22,222,222 \times 9 = ?$

💡 **Think**

✏️ **Solve**

⭐ **Answer**

3. Given ▢ = 2, ◯ = 4, and △ = 6, fill in the blanks below with the same number to make the statement true.

▢ + ◯ + △ = _____ × ▢ × △ − _____ × ▢ × ◯

💡 **Think**

✏️ **Solve**

⭐ **Answer**

4. Given the following statements:

$$11 \times 11 = 121$$
$$111 \times 111 = 12,321$$
$$1,111 \times 1,111 = 1,234,321$$

What is the result of 11,111,111 × 11,111,111?

💡 **Think**

✏️ **Solve**

⭐ **Answer**

Skill Set 6: Work Backward

Working backward is a strategy that makes use of the end result of a problem to find what it begins with. Very often, answers can be found by tracing back the steps and reversing the operations.

Example:

Mia saved up some money for shopping. Her mother gave her $150 more. At a shop, Mia spent $80 on a bag and half of the remaining money on a pair of shoes. She was then left with $55. How much money did Mia save up?

💡 **Think**
- Money left: $55
- Work backward by reversing the operations.

✏️ **Solve**

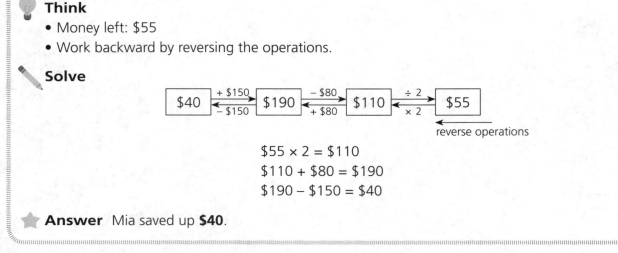

$55 × 2 = $110
$110 + $80 = $190
$190 − $150 = $40

⭐ **Answer** Mia saved up **$40**.

Give it a try!

At a farm, 2 more than half of the number of eggs were taken out from a basket. Later, 2 fewer than half of the remaining number of eggs were taken out again. If 20 eggs were left in the basket, how many eggs were there to begin with?

💡 **Think**
Work backward by reversing the operations.

✏️ **Solve**

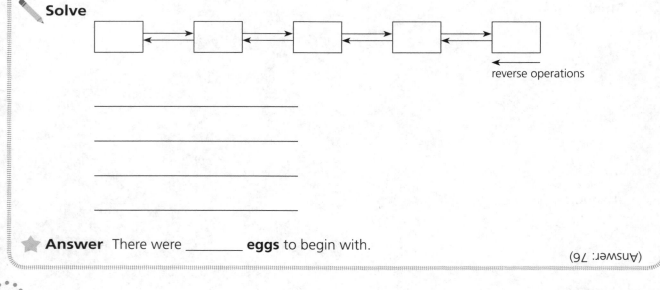

_____

_____

_____

_____

⭐ **Answer** There were _____ **eggs** to begin with.

(Answer: 76)

Practice: Work Backward

1. Samia made some fruit juice in a jug for her friends. Her friends drank 1.2 quarts of the juice before she added another 3.75 quarts of juice into the jug. Her friends then drank $\frac{1}{2}$ of the fruit juice in the jug. How much fruit juice did Samia make to begin with if 2.8 quarts of juice were left in the jug in the end?

💡 **Think**

✏️ **Solve**

⭐ **Answer**

2. Sasha made some oatmeal cookies for the weekend. She packed 36 of them into small bags and another two dozen into a container. She then gave the remaining cookies equally to her two best friends. Each of her friends received 15 cookies. How many cookies did Sasha make?

💡 **Think**

✏️ **Solve**

⭐ **Answer**

3. A is a number. Multiply A by 4 and subtract 28 from the product. Divide the result by 2. The final result is 10. What number is A?

💡 **Think**

✏️ **Solve**

⭐ **Answer**

4. X is a number. Add 2 to X and divide the sum by 3. Subtract 1 from the quotient and multiply the result by itself. The final result is 16. What number is X?

💡 **Think**

✏️ **Solve**

⭐ **Answer**

Skill Set 7: Draw a Diagram/Model

Drawing diagrams helps us "see" the relationship among the data found in a problem. This is a good and effective way to organize information and data.

Example:

A rectangular block of wood, 20 centimeters by 18 centimeters by 9 centimeters, is cut into many 3-centimeter cubes. What is the maximum number of 3-centimeter cubes that can be cut out?

💡 **Think**
- Draw a block 20 cm by 18 cm by 9 cm.
- Draw 3-cm cubes within the block.
- Solve by using the diagram.

✏️ **Solve**

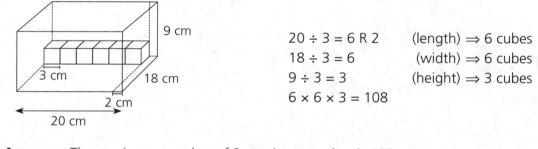

$20 \div 3 = 6 \text{ R } 2$ (length) $\Rightarrow$ 6 cubes
$18 \div 3 = 6$ (width) $\Rightarrow$ 6 cubes
$9 \div 3 = 3$ (height) $\Rightarrow$ 3 cubes
$6 \times 6 \times 3 = 108$

⭐ **Answer**   The maximum number of 3-centimeter cubes is **108**.

Give it a try!

What is the maximum number of 2-centimeter cubes that can be fitted into a rectangular box measuring 15 centimeters by 10 centimeters by 13 centimeters?

💡 **Think**
Solve by using the diagram.

✏️ **Solve**

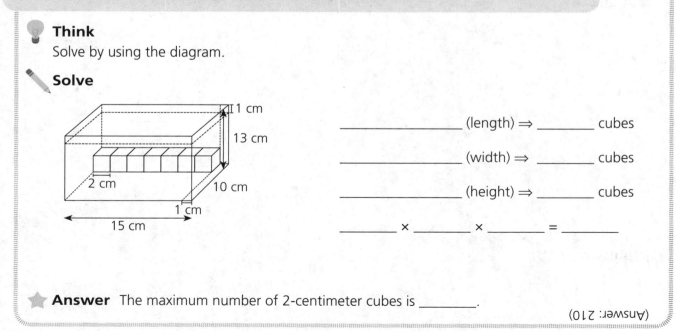

_____ (length) $\Rightarrow$ _____ cubes

_____ (width) $\Rightarrow$ _____ cubes

_____ (height) $\Rightarrow$ _____ cubes

_____ $\times$ _____ $\times$ _____ = _____

⭐ **Answer**   The maximum number of 2-centimeter cubes is _____.

(Answer: 210)

Practice: Draw a Diagram/Model

1. A class has 40 students. Of those, 28 play football, and 16 play basketball. The remaining 8 do not play football or basketball. How many students play both football and basketball?

💡 **Think**

✏️ **Solve**

⭐ **Answer**

2. Farmer John had 8 sons. Each received a plot of land as shown below. What was the total area of land that the 8 sons received?

💡 **Think**

✏️ **Solve**

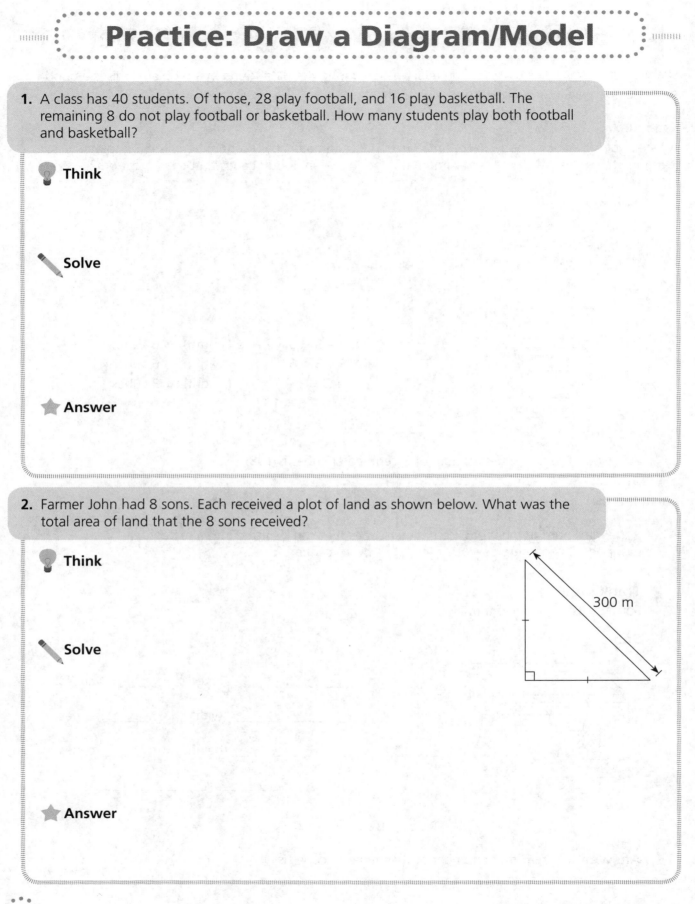

300 m

⭐ **Answer**

Practice: Draw a Diagram/Model

3. A circle is drawn inside a square with a base of 10 centimeters. A smaller square is drawn in the circle with its corners touching the edges of the bigger square. What is the area of the smaller square?

💡 **Think**

✏️ **Solve**

⭐ **Answer**

4. Alicia and Bailey have 80 beads altogether. Bailey and Candice have 70 beads altogether. Alicia and Candice have 90 beads altogether. How many beads does each girl have?

💡 **Think**

✏️ **Solve**

⭐ **Answer**

Skill Set 8: Look for a Pattern

To make sense of the data given in a problem, examine the variables to find the specific pattern. The development of the pattern leads to a solution.

Example:

Simone used some square blocks to build the figures shown below. How many square blocks does she need to build Figure 6?

💡 **Think**
- Study the figures and look for a pattern.
- Draw a table to fill in the data.
- Use the table to find the solution.

Figure 1   Figure 2   Figure 3

✏️ **Solve**

Figure	Number of blocks	Pattern
1	1	1
2	3	1 + 2
3	6	1 + 2 + 3
4	10	1 + 2 + 3 + 4
⋮	⋮	⋮
6	21	1 + 2 + 3 + 4 + 5 + 6

⭐ **Answer** Simone needs **21 square blocks** to build Figure 6.

Give it a try!

Taron built the structure shown below. How many cubes does he need to build a similar structure with 10 layers?

💡 **Think**

Draw a table and use it to find the solution.

←— Layer 1
←— Layer 2
←— Layer 3

✏️ **Solve**

Layer	Number of cubes in each layer	Pattern
1		
2		
3		
4		
⋮	⋮	⋮
10		

_____ + _____ + _____ + _____ + _____ + _____ + _____ + _____ + _____ + _____ = _____

⭐ **Answer** Taron needs _____ cubes to build the structure.

(Answer: 385)

Practice: Look for a Pattern

1. Timothy built the models shown below. How many triangular blocks does he need to build Model 7?

💡 **Think**

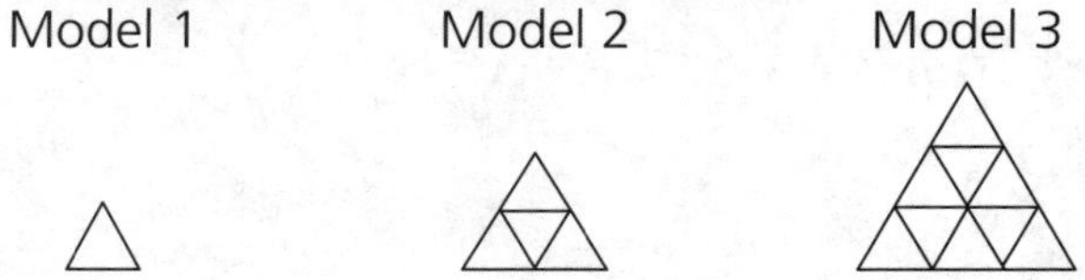

Model 1   Model 2   Model 3

✏️ **Solve**

⭐ **Answer**

2. China used some sticks to create the diagrams shown below. How many sticks does she need to create Diagram 8?

💡 **Think**

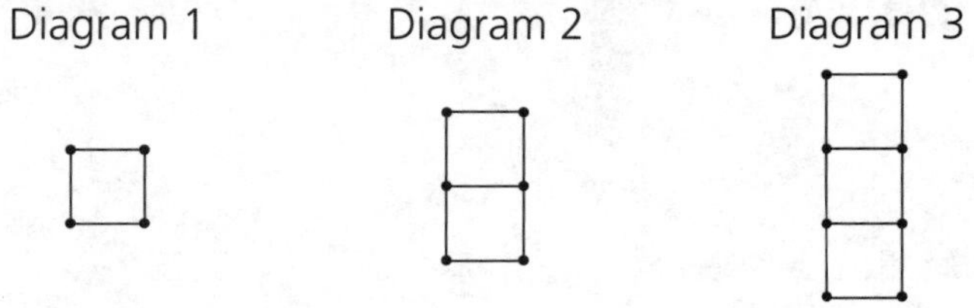

Diagram 1   Diagram 2   Diagram 3

✏️ **Solve**

⭐ **Answer**

Practice: Look for a Pattern

3. Eboni used some beads to create the figures shown below. How many beads does she need to create Figure 9?

💡 **Think**

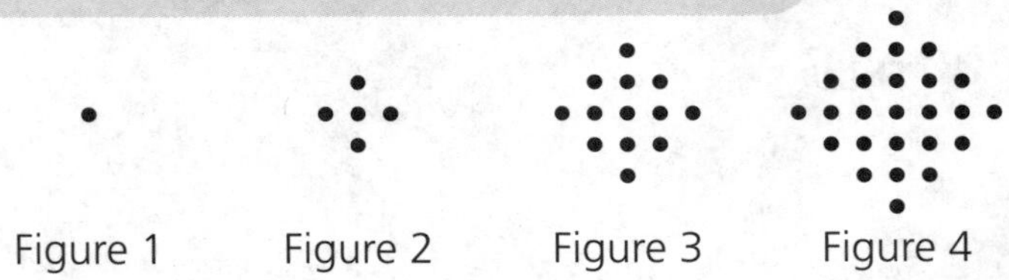

Figure 1   Figure 2   Figure 3   Figure 4

✏️ **Solve**

⭐ **Answer**

4. Study the structure shown below. How many blocks would be on Layer 8?

💡 **Think**

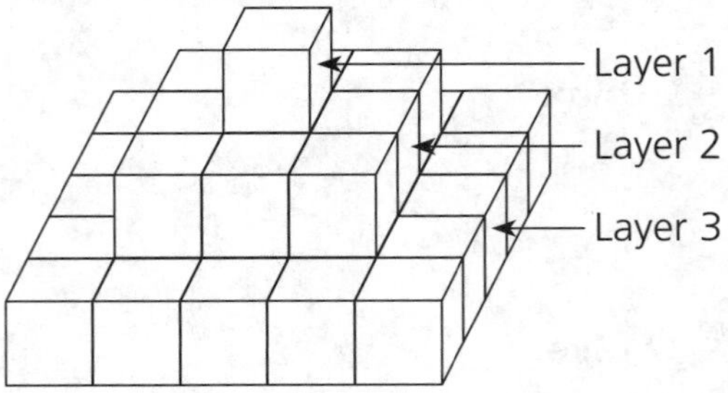

Layer 1

Layer 2

Layer 3

✏️ **Solve**

⭐ **Answer**

Skill Set 9: Make a List/Table

Making a list or a table with the given data or information helps organize the data in an orderly manner. This makes it possible to see missing data or recognize patterns.

Example:

Mrs. Toma bought some stickers for her students. If she gave each student 4 stickers, she would be 1 sticker short. If she gave each student 3 stickers, she would have 8 stickers left. How many students did she have altogether?

Think
- Data given: 4 stickers → 1 short (multiple of 4 less 1), 3 stickers → 8 left (multiple of 3 plus 8)
- List the multiples of 3 and 4.
- Find the common number.

Solve

Possible number of students:	1	2	3	4	5	6	7	8	(9)
Multiples of 4:	4	8	12	16	20	24	28	32	36
1 short:	3	7	11	15	19	23	27	31	(35)
Multiples of 3:	3	6	9	12	15	18	21	24	27
8 left:	11	14	17	20	23	26	29	32	(35)

Answer She had **9 students** altogether.

Give it a try!

Two empty tanks are being filled with water. Water flows into tank A at a rate of 15 liters per minute for 3 minutes. After 3 minutes, water flows into tank B at a rate of 20 liters per minute. How long will it take for the two tanks to have 220 liters of water altogether?

Think
Make a table and use it to find the solution.

Solve

	0 min.	1 min.	2 min.						
Tank A	0	15 L							
Tank B	0	0							
Total	0	15 L							

Answer It will take _____ **minutes** for the two tanks to have 220 liters of water altogether.

(Answer: 8)

Practice: Make a List/Table

1. Jayla distributed some pebbles to her friends. If she gave 6 pebbles to each friend, she would be 2 pebbles short. If she gave 5 pebbles to each friend, she would have 5 pebbles left. How many pebbles did Jayla have altogether?

💡 **Think**

✏️ **Solve**

⭐ **Answer**

2. A delivery company charged $3 for every package it delivered safely, but it would pay a penalty of $30 for every package it lost. In a certain week, the company was paid $183 for their services. If 3 packages were lost, how many packages were delivered safely?

💡 **Think**

✏️ **Solve**

⭐ **Answer**

3. Car A leaves town X at 8 A.M. and travels at 60 mph. Car B leaves town X 2 hours later and travels at 80 mph in the same direction. At what time does car B catch up with car A?

💡 **Think**

✏️ **Solve**

⭐ **Answer**

4. Chase has 3 different colors of counters: blue, red, and yellow. He can make different codes by using at least 1 counter. How many different codes can Chase make altogether?

💡 **Think**

✏️ **Solve**

⭐ **Answer**

Skill Set 10: Guess and Check

Guess and check refers to making calculated guesses and deriving a solution from them. It is a popular heuristic skill that is often used for upper primary mathematical problems. Because the guesses at the solutions can be checked immediately, the answers are always correct.

Example:

Lucy was reading a book and stopped at 2 facing pages. The product of the 2 page numbers was 156. What were the page numbers?

💡 **Think**
- Data: 2 page numbers are consecutive, product = 156
- Make guesses and list them.
- Check the solution and confirm the answer.

✏️ **Solve**

Guess 1: $10 \times 11 = 110$ ✘
Guess 2: $11 \times 12 = 132$ ✘
Guess 3: $12 \times 13 = 156$ ✓

⭐ **Answer** The page numbers were **12** and **13**.

Give it a try!

Seth had some $1 bills and $5 bills. The ratio of his $1 bills to his $5 bills was 7:2. If Seth had a total of $68, how many bills did he have altogether?

💡 **Think**

Make guesses and list them.

✏️ **Solve**

$1	$5	sum	
× 7 = $7	× 2 = $10	$17	✘

Number of $1 bills → _____

Number of $5 bills → _____

Total number of bills → _____ + _____ = _____

⭐ **Answer** He had _____ **bills** altogether.

Practice: Guess and Check

1. Amy rolled a six-sided die 3 times in a row. She made note of the number that appeared on the top side of the die each time. What were the 3 numbers that Amy rolled if their product was 100?

💡 **Think**

✏️ **Solve**

⭐ **Answer**

2. Amelia bought 90 stickers to decorate some cards. Each sticker cost either 5¢ or 10¢. If she paid $5.70 in all for the stickers, how many 5¢ stickers did Amelia buy?

💡 **Think**

✏️ **Solve**

⭐ **Answer**

Practice: Guess and Check

3. A farmer raises fowl and cattle. He has more fowl than cattle. If the animals have 110 legs altogether, how many fowl and how many cattle are there?

💡 **Think**

✏️ **Solve**

⭐ **Answer**

4. The ages of 3 brothers are consecutive even numbers. If the sum of their ages is 60, what are their ages?

💡 **Think**

✏️ **Solve**

⭐ **Answer**

Skill Set 11: Before and After

Before and After is often used to solve problems with two scenarios. By putting the data into before and after diagrams or mathematical representations, and then doing a comparison, a solution can be derived easily.

Example:

Mr. Unger had some American stamps and European stamps. The number of American stamps was $\frac{2}{3}$ that of European stamps. He gave some American stamps away, and the number of American stamps became $\frac{2}{5}$ that of European stamps. If he had 200 American stamps to begin with, how many of them did he give away?

Think

• Data: American stamps given away, European stamps remained unchanged.
• Make the ratio for European stamps the same before and after American stamps were given away.
• Solve by using the unitary method.

Solve

Before	After
Am : Eu	Am : Eu
2 : 3 ⟍ ×5	2 : 5 ⟍ ×3
10 : (15)	6 : (15)

10 − 6 = 4 units (American stamps given away)
10 units → 200
1 unit → 200 ÷ 10 = 20
4 units → 20 × 4 = 80

Answer He gave away **80 American stamps**.

Give it a try!

Peter bought a total of 75 $2 stamps and $5 stamps. The number of $5 stamps was $\frac{2}{10}$ the total number of stamps. Peter used some $5 stamps, and the number of $5 stamps became $\frac{1}{6}$ the total number of stamps. How many $5 stamps did Peter use?

Think

Solve by using the unitary method.

Solve

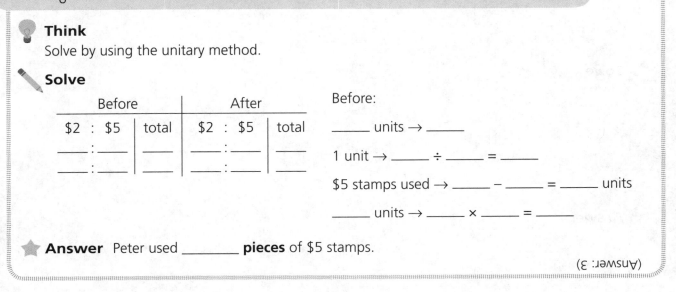

Before			After		
$2 : $5	total		$2 : $5	total	
___ : ___	___		___ : ___	___	
___ : ___	___		___ : ___	___	

Before:

_____ units → _____

1 unit → _____ ÷ _____ = _____

$5 stamps used → _____ − _____ = _____ units

_____ units → _____ × _____ = _____

Answer Peter used _____ **pieces** of $5 stamps.

(Answer: 3)

Practice: Before and After

1. Jawan had some blue and red marbles at a ratio of 2:7. When he bought some more blue marbles, the new ratio became 17:28. If he had 8 blue marbles to begin with, how many blue marbles did Jawan buy?

💡 **Think**

✏️ **Solve**

⭐ **Answer**

2. The number of boys, girls, and adults at a marathon was at a ratio of 5:8:2. When some girls left the marathon, the new ratio became 10:9:4. If 150 people participated altogether, how many girls left the marathon?

💡 **Think**

✏️ **Solve**

⭐ **Answer**

3. A sports complex has basketballs and footballs. The number of basketballs is $\frac{5}{7}$ the total number of balls. If 45 basketballs are damaged and thrown away and the number of remaining basketballs is now $\frac{1}{2}$ the total number of balls, what is the total number of balls left?

💡 **Think**

✏️ **Solve**

⭐ **Answer**

4. A total of 1,023 guppies and angelfish were in a big tank. The number of guppies was $\frac{9}{11}$ the total number of fish in the tank. However, some angelfish were sold, and the number of guppies became $\frac{27}{31}$ the total number of fish. How many angelfish were sold?

💡 **Think**

✏️ **Solve**

⭐ **Answer**

Skill Set 12: Make Suppositions

Making suppositions is another higher-order heuristic skill that is often used for upper primary mathematical problems. It requires one to make an assumption to a given problem before attempting to solve it.

Example:
A farmer has 60 chickens and cows. They have a total of 144 legs. How many chickens does the farmer have?

💡 **Think**
- Make assumptions that the farmer has either all chickens or all cows.
- Look for shortage or excess of legs and solve accordingly.

✏️ **Solve**
Assuming all are chickens:

total number of legs = $60 \times 2 = 120$

difference in total number of legs → $144 - 120 = 24$ (excess)

difference in number of legs of chicken and cow → $4 - 2 = 2$

cows → $24 \div 2 = 12$

chickens → $60 - 12 = 48$

⭐ **Answer** The farmer has **48 chickens**.

Give it a try!

Another farmer has 70 chickens and cows. They have a total of 240 legs. How many cows does the farmer have?

💡 **Think**
Again look for shortage or excess of legs and solve accordingly.

✏️ **Solve**
Assuming all are cows:

total number of legs = _____ × _____ = _____

difference in total number of legs = _____ − _____ = _____

difference in number of legs of chicken and cow = _____ − _____ = _____ (   )

chickens → _____ ÷ _____ = _____

cows → _____ − _____ = _____

⭐ **Answer** The farmer has _____ **cows**.

(Answer: 50)

Practice: Make Suppositions

1. Zach has 50 5¢ coins and 10¢ coins. The total value of the coins is $3.30. How many 5¢ coins does Zach have?

💡 **Think**

✏️ **Solve**

⭐ **Answer**

2. There are 50 beetles and spiders in a tank. They have a total of 328 legs. How many beetles are in the tank?

💡 **Think**

✏️ **Solve**

⭐ **Answer**

Practice: Make Suppositions

3. A school paid $434 for admission tickets to a museum for 101 students and teachers. If an adult ticket cost $6 and a student ticket cost $4, how many adult tickets did the school buy?

💡 **Think**

✏️ **Solve**

⭐ **Answer**

4. Vanessa packed 255 cookies into a total of 20 boxes. A box can contain 12 cookies or 15 cookies. How many boxes of 12 cookies did Vanessa pack?

💡 **Think**

✏️ **Solve**

⭐ **Answer**

5. An office manager purchased 37 calendars and organizers for $367.50. If each calendar cost $6.80 and each organizer cost $12.90, how many organizers did the manager purchase?

💡 **Think**

✏️ **Solve**

 Answer

Mixed Practice: Easy

1. The cost of a glass jar filled with orange juice was $4.50. The cost of the same glass jar filled with water was $2.30. The cost of orange juice was 3 times that of water. What was the cost of the empty glass jar?

💡 **Think**

✏️ **Solve**

⭐ **Answer**

2. The total capacity of 3 containers, X, Y, and Z, is 600 pints. Y can hold 12 pints more than X, while Z can hold 4 times as much as Y. What is the capacity of Y?

💡 **Think**

✏️ **Solve**

⭐ **Answer**

Mixed Practice: Easy

3. Yvonne labeled chairs in a hall from 1 to 100. How many digits did she use to complete the task?

💡 **Think**

✏️ **Solve**

⭐ **Answer**

4. Mrs. Tanaka paid a total of $4.35 for 1 pear, 2 apples, and 4 oranges. The price of 1 pear and 1 apple was $1.25. The price of 1 apple and 1 orange was $1.00. What was the price of 4 oranges?

💡 **Think**

✏️ **Solve**

⭐ **Answer**

5. Matt spent $55 at a bookstore. He then spent $\frac{1}{3}$ of his remaining money at a toy shop. After withdrawing $80 from the ATM, he had $120 with him. How much money did Matt have to begin with?

💡 **Think**

✏️ **Solve**

⭐ **Answer**

6. A 200-liter oil tank is to be filled with oil from tap A and tap B. Oil flows out of tap A into the tank at 3 liters per minute and flows out of tap B into the tank at 5 liters per minute. If tap B is only turned on 1.5 minutes after tap A is turned on, how long does it take for the tank to be completely filled? Give your answer to the nearest minute.

💡 **Think**

✏️ **Solve**

⭐ **Answer**

7. Mr. Ahmed is 29 years old. His daughter is 5 years old. In how many years' time will Mr. Ahmed be 4 times as old as his daughter?

💡 **Think**

✏️ **Solve**

⭐ **Answer**

8. Jordana and Wendy had stickers at a ratio of 4:5. After Jordana gave 60 stickers away, the new ratio became 3:10. How many stickers did Wendy have?

💡 **Think**

✏️ **Solve**

⭐ **Answer**

9. James selected 3 different number cards from 1 to 10. If the product of the 3 numbers was 189, what were the 3 number cards James selected?

💡 **Think**

✏️ **Solve**

⭐ **Answer**

10. A parking lot has 50 cars and motorcycles. If the vehicles have 144 wheels altogether, how many cars are in the parking lot?

💡 **Think**

✏️ **Solve**

⭐ **Answer**

Mixed Practice: Intermediate

1. Scott, Rashad, and Caleb had 144 coins altogether. When Scott gave some of his coins to Rashad, the number of coins Rashad had doubled. Rashad then gave some of his coins to Caleb, and the number of coins Caleb had also doubled. If the 3 boys had the same number of coins in the end, how many coins did each boy have to begin with?

💡 **Think**

✏️ **Solve**

⭐ **Answer**

2. Two groups of students went to the Science Center. Group A had 18 more students than group B. When 9 students from group B joined group A, the number of students in group A became 3 times the number of students in group B. How many students were in both groups?

💡 **Think**

✏️ **Solve**

⭐ **Answer**

3. A city plans to hold a sweepstakes. For the first prize, 1 winner will be picked. For the second prize, 3 winners will be picked. For every subsequent prize, 2 more than the previous number of winners will be picked. If 10 prizes are awarded in all, how many winners will be picked at the end of the sweepstakes?

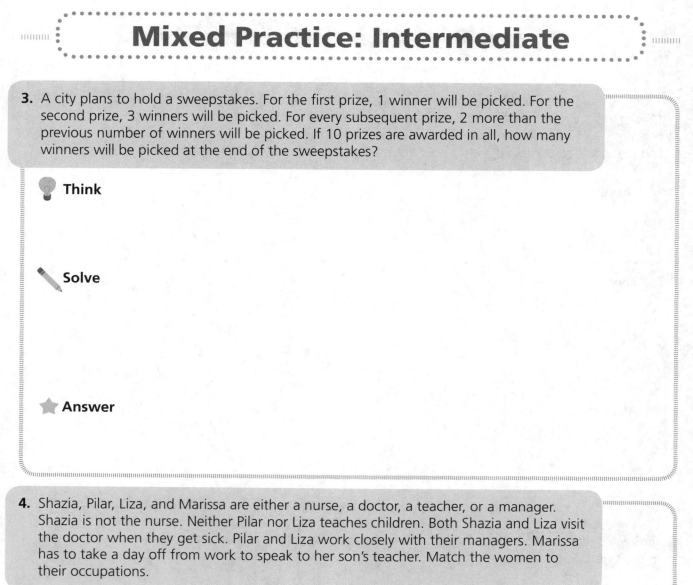

Think

Solve

Answer

4. Shazia, Pilar, Liza, and Marissa are either a nurse, a doctor, a teacher, or a manager. Shazia is not the nurse. Neither Pilar nor Liza teaches children. Both Shazia and Liza visit the doctor when they get sick. Pilar and Liza work closely with their managers. Marissa has to take a day off from work to speak to her son's teacher. Match the women to their occupations.

Think

Solve

Answer

5. Charisma brought some money for an overseas trip. She used 20% of her money on food. She then spent $\frac{2}{3}$ of her remaining money on shopping. Finally, she used $\frac{1}{2}$ of what was left to pay for admission tickets to sightseeing spots. In the end, she was left with $110. How much money did Charisma bring on the trip?

💡 **Think**

✏️ **Solve**

⭐ **Answer**

6. Buses are chartered to ferry students for an excursion. If each bus takes 40 students, 20 seats will be vacant. If each bus takes 36 students, 12 students will not be able to board.
  (a) How many buses are chartered?
  (b) How many students are going on the excursion?

💡 **Think**

✏️ **Solve**

⭐ **Answer**

7. In a school, 45% of the students are boys. Of those students, 30% wear glasses, of which $\frac{1}{3}$ are black-rimmed. If 162 boys wear black-rimmed glasses, how many male and female students are in the school altogether?

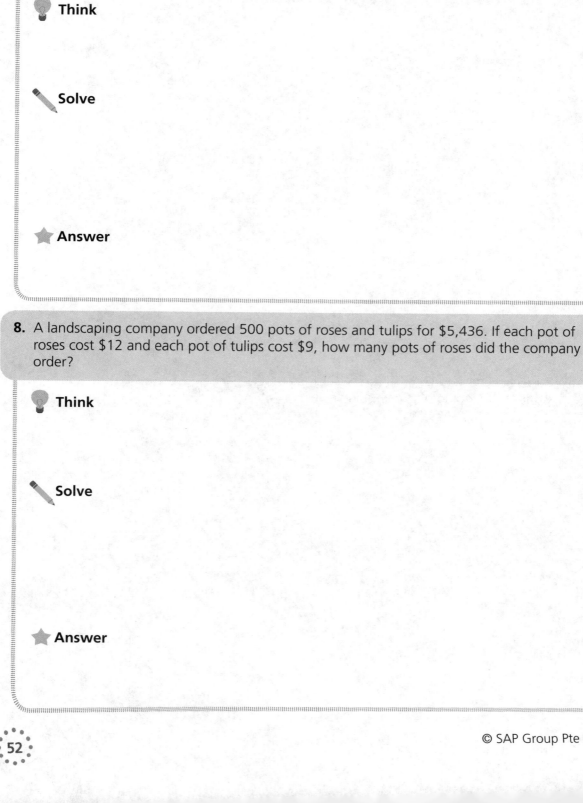

💡 **Think**

✏️ **Solve**

⭐ **Answer**

8. A landscaping company ordered 500 pots of roses and tulips for $5,436. If each pot of roses cost $12 and each pot of tulips cost $9, how many pots of roses did the company order?

💡 **Think**

✏️ **Solve**

⭐ **Answer**

9. Given the following statements:

$$1 \times 9 + 2 = 11$$
$$12 \times 9 + 3 = 111$$
$$123 \times 9 + 4 = 1{,}111$$

What is the result of $12{,}345{,}678 \times 9 + 9$?

💡 **Think**

✏️ **Solve**

⭐ **Answer**

10. Some students took a survey. 48 liked comedy, while 37 liked horror movies. If 12 liked both comedy and horror movies and 7 liked neither, how many students took the survey?

💡 **Think**

✏️ **Solve**

⭐ **Answer**

Mixed Practice: Challenging

1. The figure below is made up of overlapping squares, P, Q, and R. The ratio of the area of P to that of Q to that of R is 2:4:7. If $\frac{1}{4}$ of P is shaded, what percentage of the figure is unshaded?

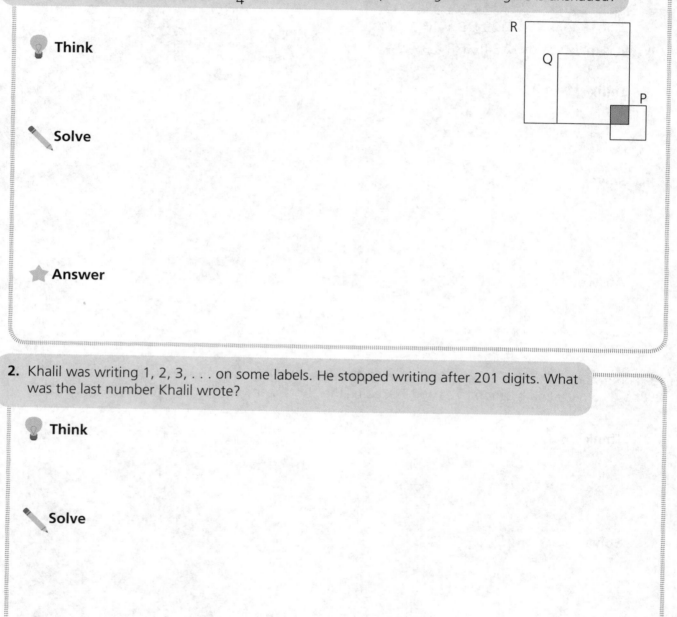

💡 **Think**

✏️ **Solve**

⭐ **Answer**

2. Khalil was writing 1, 2, 3, . . . on some labels. He stopped writing after 201 digits. What was the last number Khalil wrote?

💡 **Think**

✏️ **Solve**

⭐ **Answer**

Mixed Practice: Challenging

3. Kade is 20% heavier than Danny. Danny is 10% lighter than his sister. How much heavier is Kade than Danny's sister in terms of percentage?

💡 **Think**

✏️ **Solve**

⭐ **Answer**

4. Brad and Ben each had some money. Brad gave $\frac{1}{2}$ of what he had to Ben. Ben then gave 50% of his money to Brad. Finally, Brad gave $\frac{1}{2}$ of his money back to Ben. In the end, Brad had $96 and Ben had $228. How much money did each of the boys have to begin with?

💡 **Think**

✏️ **Solve**

⭐ **Answer**

5. Abbie, Byron, Callista, and Dawson each pick a favorite ice-cream flavor from a choice of 4 flavors: chocolate, mint, strawberry, and vanilla. The girls do not like fruit-flavored ice cream. Abbie and her brother prefer their picks to Dawson's mint ice cream. Callista does not mind sharing her girlfriend's vanilla ice cream. Which flavor of ice cream does each child pick?

💡 **Think**

✏️ **Solve**

⭐ **Answer**

6. An empty school bus picks up 2 boys and half as many girls at stop 1. It picks up another 4 girls and half as many boys at stop 2. It then continues to pick up 6 boys and half as many girls at stop 3, and so on. If the school bus has a capacity of 82, at which stop will it not be able to pick up all of the boys and girls?

💡 **Think**

✏️ **Solve**

⭐ **Answer**

7. Dad is 3 times as old as the younger daughter. Mom is twice as old as the elder daughter. If the sum of all of their ages is 130, what are their respective ages?

💡 **Think**

✏️ **Solve**

⭐ **Answer**

8. A company spent $760 in all on 5 similar computer monitors and 6 similar printers. Each monitor cost $20 more than each printer.
(a) What was the price of each monitor?
(b) What was the price of each printer?

💡 **Think**

✏️ **Solve**

⭐ **Answer**

Answer Key

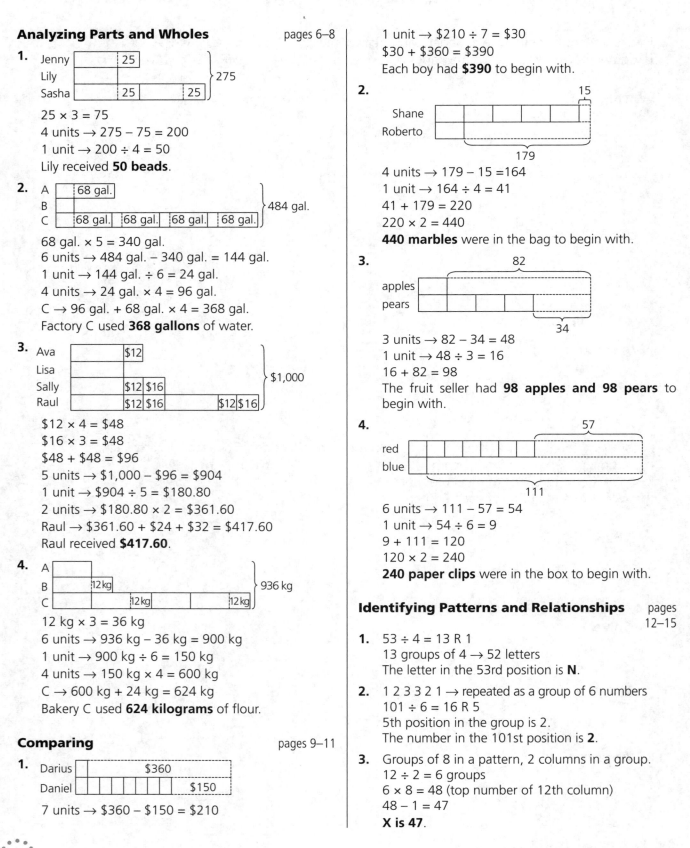

Analyzing Parts and Wholes   pages 6–8

1.
Jenny | 25
Lily
Sasha | 25 | 25
} 275

25 × 3 = 75
4 units → 275 − 75 = 200
1 unit → 200 ÷ 4 = 50
Lily received **50 beads**.

2.
A | 68 gal.
B
C | 68 gal. | 68 gal. | 68 gal. | 68 gal.
} 484 gal.

68 gal. × 5 = 340 gal.
6 units → 484 gal. − 340 gal. = 144 gal.
1 unit → 144 gal. ÷ 6 = 24 gal.
4 units → 24 gal. × 4 = 96 gal.
C → 96 gal. + 68 gal. × 4 = 368 gal.
Factory C used **368 gallons** of water.

3.
Ava | $12
Lisa
Sally | $12 | $16
Raul | $12 | $16 | $12 | $16
} $1,000

$12 × 4 = $48
$16 × 3 = $48
$48 + $48 = $96
5 units → $1,000 − $96 = $904
1 unit → $904 ÷ 5 = $180.80
2 units → $180.80 × 2 = $361.60
Raul → $361.60 + $24 + $32 = $417.60
Raul received **$417.60**.

4.
A
B | 12 kg
C | 12 kg | 12 kg
} 936 kg

12 kg × 3 = 36 kg
6 units → 936 kg − 36 kg = 900 kg
1 unit → 900 kg ÷ 6 = 150 kg
4 units → 150 kg × 4 = 600 kg
C → 600 kg + 24 kg = 624 kg
Bakery C used **624 kilograms** of flour.

Comparing   pages 9–11

1.
Darius | $360
Daniel | | | | | | | $150

7 units → $360 − $150 = $210

1 unit → $210 ÷ 7 = $30
$30 + $360 = $390
Each boy had **$390** to begin with.

2.
Shane | | | | | | 15
Roberto
179

4 units → 179 − 15 = 164
1 unit → 164 ÷ 4 = 41
41 + 179 = 220
220 × 2 = 440
440 marbles were in the bag to begin with.

3.
82
apples
pears
34

3 units → 82 − 34 = 48
1 unit → 48 ÷ 3 = 16
16 + 82 = 98
The fruit seller had **98 apples and 98 pears** to begin with.

4.
57
red
blue
111

6 units → 111 − 57 = 54
1 unit → 54 ÷ 6 = 9
9 + 111 = 120
120 × 2 = 240
240 paper clips were in the box to begin with.

Identifying Patterns and Relationships   pages 12–15

1.
53 ÷ 4 = 13 R 1
13 groups of 4 → 52 letters
The letter in the 53rd position is **N**.

2.
1 2 3 3 2 1 → repeated as a group of 6 numbers
101 ÷ 6 = 16 R 5
5th position in the group is 2.
The number in the 101st position is **2**.

3.
Groups of 8 in a pattern, 2 columns in a group.
12 ÷ 2 = 6 groups
6 × 8 = 48 (top number of 12th column)
48 − 1 = 47
X is 47.

4. 3 A T H 5 → repeated as a group of 5 digits and letters
88 ÷ 5 = 17 R 3
3rd position in the group is T.
The letter in the 88th position is **T**.

5. Groups of 12 in a pattern, 2 rows in a group.
69 ÷ 12 = 5 R 9
9 − 6 = 3 (3rd position from the right)
I would expect to find 69 in **column D**.

Deduction

pages 16–18

1. Ellen is opposite Jill → P or R belongs to Ellen or Jill, and Q belongs to Felipe.
Ellen is left of Felipe → R belongs to Ellen, and P belongs to Jill.

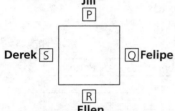

2.

	red	orange	blue	black	white
Jaime		✓	✗	✗	
Kate	✓				
Lamonte	✗	✗			✓
Marcus				✓	
Nathan			✓		

3. A finishes before E only and just behind C → A is 4th, E is 5th, and C is 3rd
No team before B → B is 1st

	1st	2nd	3rd	4th	5th
A				✓	
B	✓				
C			✓		
D		✓			
E					✓

4. Mr. Taylor is older than the lawyer → Mr. Taylor is not the lawyer.
Mr. Lewis and the doctor are not of the same age → Mr. Lewis is not the doctor.
The doctor is younger than Mr. Lang → Mr. Lang is not the doctor.

	doctor	lawyer	teacher
Mr. Lewis	✗	✓	
Mr. Lang	✗	✗	✓
Mr. Taylor	✓	✗	

Mr. Taylor (doctor) is older than the lawyer, and the doctor is younger than Mr. Lang → Mr. Lang is not the lawyer.
Mr. Lang is the teacher.

Induction

pages 19–21

1. Since ◇ + □ = 16 + 4 = 20,
20 = ___ × △ − ___ × □
   = ___ × 8 − ___ × 4
Since 8 = 4 + 4,
20 = ___ × (4 + 4) − ___ × 4
20 = ___ × 4 + ___ × 4 − ___ × 4
20 = ___ × 4
___ = 20 ÷ 4
    = 5
So, ◇ + □ = **5** × △ − **5** × □.

2.

	2s in factor	9s in answer
Statement 1:	1	0
Statement 2:	2	1
Statement 3:	3	2
Statement 4:	4	3
⋮	⋮	⋮
Statement 8:	8	7

The number of 2s in the factor is always 1 more than the number of 9s in the answer.
So, 22,222,222 × 9 = **199,999,998**.

3. Since □ + ○ + △ = 2 + 4 + 6 = 12,
12 = ___ × □ × △ − ___ × □ × ○
   = ___ × 2 × 6 − ___ × 2 × 4
   = ___ × 12 − ___ × 8
Since 12 = 4 + 8,
12 = ___ × (4 + 8) − ___ × 8
12 = ___ × 4 + ___ × 8 − ___ × 8
12 = ___ × 4
___ = 12 ÷ 4
    = 3
So, □ + ○ + △ = **3** × □ × △ − **3** × □ × ○.

4.
11 × 11 = 1 2 1
111 × 111 = 12,321
1,111 × 1,111 = 1,234,321
11,111,111 → 8 1s
So, 11,111,111 × 11,111,111 = **123,456,787,654,321**.

Work Backward

pages 22–24

1. 2.8 quarts × 2 = 5.6 quarts
5.6 quarts − 3.75 quarts = 1.85 quarts
1.85 quarts + 1.2 quarts = 3.05 quarts
Samia made **3.05 quarts** of fruit juice to begin with.

2. 15 × 2 = 30
30 + 24 + 36 = 90
Sasha made **90 cookies**.

3. 10 × 2 = 20

20 + 28 = 48
48 ÷ 4 = 12
A is 12.

4. 16 = 4 × 4
4 + 1 = 5
5 × 3 = 15
15 − 2 = 13
X is 13.

Draw a Diagram/Model

pages 25–27

1.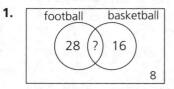

28 + 16 + 8 = 52
52 − 40 = 12
Check: 12 + (28 − 12) + (16 − 12) + 8 = 40
12 students play both football and basketball.

2.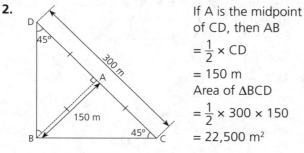

If A is the midpoint of CD, then AB

$= \frac{1}{2} \times CD$

= 150 m

Area of ΔBCD

$= \frac{1}{2} \times 300 \times 150$

= 22,500 m²

1 plot → 22,500 m²
8 plots → 22,500 × 8 = 180,000 m²
The total area of land that the 8 sons received was **180,000 m²**.

3.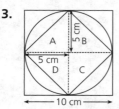

Divide the smaller square into 4 equal triangles.
Area of smaller square
= Area of A + area of B + area of C + area of D
$= 4 \times \frac{1}{2} \times 5 \times 5$
= 50 cm²
or
Area of smaller square
$= \frac{1}{2} \times$ area of bigger square
$= \frac{1}{2} \times 10 \times 10$
= 50 cm²
The area of the smaller square is **50 cm²**.

4.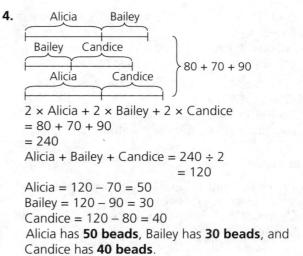

2 × Alicia + 2 × Bailey + 2 × Candice
= 80 + 70 + 90
= 240
Alicia + Bailey + Candice = 240 ÷ 2
= 120

Alicia = 120 − 70 = 50
Bailey = 120 − 90 = 30
Candice = 120 − 80 = 40
Alicia has **50 beads**, Bailey has **30 beads**, and Candice has **40 beads**.

Look for a Pattern

pages 28–30

1.

Model	Number of △s	Pattern
1	1	1
2	4	2 × 2
3	9	3 × 3
4	16	4 × 4
⋮	⋮	⋮
7	49	7 × 7

He needs **49 triangular blocks** to build Model 7.

2.

Diagram	No. of sticks	Pattern
1	4	4
2	7	4 + 3 × 1
3	10	4 + 3 × 2
4	13	4 + 3 × 3
⋮	⋮	⋮
8	25	4 + 3 × 7

She needs **25 sticks** to create Diagram 8.

3.

Figure	No. of beads	Pattern
1	1	1
2	5	2 × 2 + 1 × 1
3	13	3 × 3 + 2 × 2
4	25	4 × 4 + 3 × 3
⋮	⋮	⋮
9	145	9 × 9 + 8 × 8

She needs **145 beads** to create Figure 9.

4.

Layer	No. of blocks	Pattern
1	1	1 × 1
2	9	3 × 3
3	25	5 × 5
⋮	⋮	⋮
8	225	15 × 15

225 blocks would be on Layer 8.

Make a List/Table

1. Multiples of 6: 6 12 18 24 30 36 42
 2 short: 4 10 16 22 28 34 ㊵
Multiples of 5: 5 10 15 20 25 30 35
 5 left: 10 15 20 25 30 35 ㊵
Jayla had **40 pebbles** altogether.

2.

Safe packages	× $3	Lost packages	× $30	Payment	Check
100	$300	3	$90	$300 − $90 = $210	✘
90	$270	3	$90	$270 − $90 = $180	✘
91	$273	3	$90	$273 − $90 = $183	✓

91 packages were delivered safely.

3.

	8 A.M.	9 A.M.	10 A.M.	11 A.M.	12 P.M.	1 P.M.	2 P.M.	3 P.M.	4 P.M.
Car A	0	60 mi.	120 mi.	180 mi.	240 mi.	300 mi.	360 mi.	420 mi.	480 mi.
Car B	0	0	0	80 mi.	160 mi.	240 mi.	320 mi.	400 mi.	480 mi.

Car B catches up with car A at **4 P.M.**

4. Using 1 counter: B, R, Y
Using 2 counters: BR, RY, BY, RB, YR, YB
Using 3 counters: BRY, BYR, RBY, RYB, YBR, YRB
Chase can make **15 codes** altogether.

Guess and Check
pages 34–36

1.

1st roll	2nd roll	3rd roll	product	
1	4	6	24	✘
3	4	5	60	✘
4	5	5	100	✓

The 3 numbers that Amy rolled were **4**, **5**, and **5**.

2.

5¢	10¢	sum	
× 45 = $2.25	× 45 = $4.50	$6.75	✘
× 55 = $2.75	× 35 = $3.50	$6.25	✘
× 65 = $3.25	× 25 = $2.50	$5.75	✘
× 66 = $3.30	× 24 = $2.40	$5.70	✓

Amelia bought **66 5¢ stickers**.
(Accept all other possible answers.)

3. fowl → 2 legs; cattle → 4 legs

2 legs	4 legs	total	
× 30 = 60	× 20 = 80	140	✘
× 20 = 40	× 10 = 40	80	✘
× 25 = 50	× 15 = 60	110	✓

There are **25 fowl** and **15 cattle**.
(Accept all other possible answers.)

4.

b1	b2	b3	sum	
14	16	18	48	✘
16	18	20	54	✘
18	20	22	60	✓

Their ages are **18**, **20**, and **22**.

Before and After
pages 37–39

1.

Before	After
b : r	b : r
2 : 7	
8 : ㉘ ×4	17 : ㉘

Before:
blue: 8 units → 8
  1 unit → 8 ÷ 8 = 1
After:
Bought → 17 − 8 = 9 units
blue: 9 units → 1 × 9 = 9
Jawan bought **9 blue marbles**.

2.

Before	After
b : g : a	b : g : a
5 : 8 : 2	
⑩ : 16 : ④ ×2	⑩ : 9 : ④

Before:
10 + 16 + 4 = 30 units
30 units → 150
1 unit → 150 ÷ 30 = 5
After:
girls left → 16 − 9 = 7 units
7 units → 5 × 7 = 35
35 girls left the marathon.

3.

Before			After		
b :	f	total	b :	f	total
5 :	②	7	2 :	②	4

basketballs thrown away → 5 − 2 = 3 units
3 units → 45
1 unit → 45 ÷ 3 = 15
4 units → 15 × 4 = 60
The total number of balls left is **60**.

4.

Before			After		
g :	a	total	g :	a	total
9 :	2	11			
㉗ :	6 ×3	33	㉗ :	4	31

Before:
33 units → 1,023
1 unit → 1,023 ÷ 33 = 31
angelfish sold → 6 − 4 = 2 units
2 units → 31 × 2 = 62
62 angelfish were sold.

Make Suppositions
pages 40–43

1. Assuming all are 5¢ coins:
50 × $0.05 = $2.50

© SAP Group Pte Ltd • FS-704118

difference in total amount → $3.30 − $2.50
                             = $0.80 (excess)
difference in value of 10¢ and 5¢
→ 10¢ − 5¢ = 5¢
10¢ coins → $0.80 ÷ $0.05 = 16
5¢ coins → 50 − 16 = 34
Zach has **34 5¢ coins**.

2. Assuming all are beetles:
    50 × 6 = 300
    difference in total number of legs → 328 − 300
                                       = 28 (excess)
    difference in number of legs of beetle and spider
    → 8 − 6 = 2
    spiders → 28 ÷ 2 = 14
    beetles → 50 − 14 = 36
    36 beetles are in the tank.

3. Assuming all were student tickets:
    101 × $4 = $404
    difference in total amount → $434 − $404
                               = $30 (excess)
    difference in value of adult and student tickets
    → $6 − $4 = $2
    adult tickets → $30 ÷ $2 = 15
    The school bought **15 adult tickets**.

4. Assuming all were boxes of 12 cookies:
    20 × 12 = 240
    difference in total amount → 255 − 240
                               = 15 (excess)
    difference in quantity of cookies in the two types of
    packing → 15 − 12 = 3
    boxes of 15 cookies → 15 ÷ 3 = 5
    boxes of 12 cookies → 20 − 5 = 15
    Vanessa packed **15 boxes of 12 cookies**.

5. Assuming all were calendars:
    37 × $6.80 = $251.60
    difference in total cost → $367.50 − $251.60
                             = $115.90 (excess)
    difference in cost of calendar and organizer
    → $12.90 − $6.80 = $6.10
    organizers → $115.90 ÷ $6.10 = 19
    The manager purchased **19 organizers**.

Mixed Practice: Easy

pages 44–48

1.
    2 units → $4.50 − $2.30 = $2.20
    1 unit → $2.20 ÷ 2 = $1.10 (water)
    $2.30 − $1.10 = $1.20

    The cost of the empty glass jar was **$1.20**.

2.
    12 pt. × 5 = 60 pt.
    6 units → 600 pt. − 60 pt. = 540 pt.
    1 unit → 540 pt. ÷ 6 = 90 pt.
    90 pt. + 12 pt. = 102 pt.
    The capacity of Y is **102 pints.**

3. 1 to 9   → 9 × 1 digit = 9 digits
    10 to 99 → 90 × 2 digits = 180 digits
    100   → 1 × 3 digits = 3 digits
    9 + 180 + 3 = 192
    She used **192 digits**.

4. 1 p + 1 a → $1.25
    1 a + 1 o → $1.00
    1 p + 2 a + 1 o → $2.25
    1 p + 2 a + 4 o → $4.35
          3 o → $4.35 − $2.25
              = $2.10
          1 o → $2.10 ÷ 3
              = $0.70
          4 o → $0.70 × 4
              = $2.80
    The price of 4 oranges was **$2.80**.

5. $120 − $80 = $40
    $40 ÷ 2 = $20
    $20 × 3 = $60
    $60 + $55 = $115
    Matt had **$115** to begin with.

6.
minute	0	1	2	3	⋯	19	22	25	26
Tap A	0	3	6	9	⋯	57	66	75	78
Tap B	0	0	2.5	7.5	⋯	87.5	102.5	117.5	122.5
total	0	3	8.5	16.5	⋯	144.5	168.5	192.5	200.5

It takes **26 minutes** for the tank to be completely filled.

7.
Year(s) from now	Mr. Ahmed	daughter	Check
1	30	6	$\frac{30}{6} \neq 4$ ✗
2	31	7	$\frac{31}{7} \neq 4$ ✗
3	32	8	$\frac{32}{8} = 4$ ✓

Mr. Ahmed will be 4 times as old as his daughter in **3 years' time**.

8.

Before			After		
J	:	W	J	:	W
4	:	5			
8	:	10	3	:	10

×2 (from 4:5 to 8:10)

Gave away → 8 − 3 = 5 units
5 units → 60
1 unit → 60 ÷ 5 = 12
10 units → 12 × 10 = 120
Wendy had **120 stickers**.

9.

1st card	2nd card	3rd card	product	
3	5	8	120	✗
3	6	9	162	✗
3	7	9	189	✓

The 3 number cards were **3**, **7**, and **9**.

10. Assuming all are cars:
50 × 4 = 200
difference in total number of wheels
→ 200 − 144
= 56 (shortage)
difference in number of wheels of a car and
motorcycle → 4 − 2 = 2
motorcycles → 56 ÷ 2 = 28
cars → 50 − 28 = 22
22 cars are in the parking lot.

Mixed Practice: Intermediate   pages 49–53

1. 144 ÷ 3 = 48
Working Backward:
Caleb

$$24 \xrightarrow{\times 2} 48$$
(÷ 2 reverse)

from Rashad

Rashad

$$36 \xrightarrow{\times 2} 72 \xrightarrow{-24} 48$$
(÷ 2, + 24 reverse)

from Scott

Scott → 144 − 24 − 36 = 84
Scott had **84 coins**, Rashad had **36 coins**, and Caleb
had **24 coins** to begin with.

2.

A: 1 unit | 9 | 18 | 9 (2 units spans 18 and part)
B: 1 unit | 9

2 units → 9 + 18 + 9 = 36
1 unit → 36 ÷ 2 = 18
4 units → 18 × 4 = 72
72 students were in both groups.

3.

Prize	No. of winners	Total	Pattern
1st	1	1	1 × 1
2nd	3	4	2 × 2
3rd	5	9	3 × 3
4th	7	16	4 × 4
⋮	⋮	⋮	⋮
10th	19	100	10 × 10

100 winners will be picked at the end of the sweepstakes.

4.

	nurse	doctor	teacher	manager
Shazia	✗	✗	✓	✗
Pilar		✓	✗	✗
Liza	✓	✗	✗	✗
Marissa			✗	✓

5. $110 × 2 = $220
1 unit → $220
3 units → $220 × 3 = $660
80% → $660
100% → $\frac{\$660}{80} \times 100 = \$825$
Charisma brought **$825** on the trip.

6.
No. of buses: 1 | 2 | 3 | 4 | 5 | 6 | 7 | ⑧
Multiples of 40: 40 | 80 | 120 | 160 | 200 | 240 | 280 | 320
−20: 20 | 60 | 100 | 140 | 180 | 220 | 260 | ③⓪⓪

No. of students:
Multiples of 36: 36 | 72 | 108 | 144 | 180 | 216 | 252 | 288
+12: 48 | 84 | 120 | 156 | 192 | 228 | 264 | ③⓪⓪

(a) 8 buses are chartered.
(b) 300 students are going on the excursion.

7. black-rimmed glasses → 162
glasses → 162 × 3 = 486
boys → $\frac{486}{30} \times 100 = 1{,}620$
students → $\frac{1{,}620}{45} \times 100 = 3{,}600$

3,600 male and female students are in the school
altogether.

8. Assuming all were tulips:
500 × $9 = $4,500
difference in total cost → $5,436 − $4,500
= $936 (excess)
difference in cost of roses and tulips → $12 − $9
= $3
roses → $936 ÷ $3 = 312
The company ordered **312 pots of roses**.

9.

$$\underline{1} \times 9 + 2 = \underset{2}{1\underbrace{1}}$$

$$\underline{12} \times 9 + 3 = 1\underset{3}{1\underbrace{1}}$$

$$\underline{123} \times 9 + 4 = 1,\underset{4}{1\underbrace{11}}$$

So, $12,345,678 \times 9 + 9 \rightarrow$ 9 1s = **111,111,111**.

10.

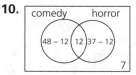

$(48 - 12) + 12 + (37 - 12) + 7 = 80$
80 students took the survey.

Mixed Practice: Challenging pages 54–57

1.

P : Q : R
2 : 4 : 7 $\Big)\times 2$
4 : 8 : 14

$\frac{1}{4}$ of P $\rightarrow$ $\frac{1}{4}$ of 4 units = 1 unit shaded.

Total units for the whole figure $\rightarrow$ 14 + (4 − 1) = 17
17 − 1 = 16
$\frac{16}{17} \times 100\% = 94\frac{2}{17}\%$
$94\frac{2}{17}$ % of the figure is unshaded.

2.

1 to 9 $\rightarrow$ 9 × 1 digit = 9 digits
10 to 99 $\rightarrow$ 90 × 2 digits = 180 digits
201 − 9 − 180 = 12 digits
100 onwards $\rightarrow$ 3 digits each
12 ÷ 3 = 4 sets of 3 digits.
So 100, 101, 102, 103.
The last number Khalil wrote was **103**.

3.

K : D   D : D's sister
120 : 100 $\Big)\div 20$ 90 : 100 $\Big)$
6 : 5 $\Big)\times 9$ $\Big)\div 2$
54 : ㊺   ㊺ : 50

K : D's sis
54 : 50 $\Big)\times 2$
108 : 100

108% − 100% = 8%
Kade is **8%** heavier than Danny's sister.

4. Working Backward:

Brad	Ben
$96 + $96	$228 − $96
$192 − $132	$132 + $132
$60 + $60	$264 − $60
$120	$204

Brad had $120 and **Ben had $204** to begin with.

5. Abbie, Callista $\rightarrow$ chocolate, vanilla
Abbie's brother is Byron.
Dawson $\rightarrow$ mint
Callista's girlfriend is Abbie $\rightarrow$ vanilla

	chocolate	mint	strawberry	vanilla
Abbie		✗	✗	✓
Byron			✓	
Callista	✓	✗	✗	
Dawson		✓		

6.

	Stop 1	Stop 2	Stop 3	Stop 4	Stop 5	Stop 6	Stop 7
boys	2	2	6	4	10	6	14
girls	1	4	3	8	5	12	7
Total	3	9	18	30	45	63	84

The school bus will not be able to pick up all of the boys and girls at **stop 7**.

7.

Dad	younger daughter	Mom	elder daughter	sum	
45	15	42	21	123	✗
51	17	46	23	137	✗
48	16	44	22	130	✓

Dad is 48 years old, **Mom is 44 years old**, the **elder daughter is 22 years old,** and the **younger daughter is 16 years old**.

8. Assuming all were monitors:
$760 + 6 × $20 = $880
5 + 6 = 11
(a) monitor $\rightarrow$ $880 ÷ 11 = $80
(b) printer $\rightarrow$ $80 − $20 = $60
The price of each monitor was **$80**, and the price of each printer was **$60**.